D0061468

# NOTHING YOU CAN'T DO!

## THE SECRET POWER OF GROWTH MINDSETS

MARY CAY RICCI

PRUFROCK PRESS INC.
WACO, TEXAS

Library of Congress catalog information
currently on file with the publisher.

Prufrock Press Inc.
P.O. Box 8813
Waco, TX 76714-8813
Phone: (800) 998-2208
Fax: (800) 240-0333
https://www.prufrock.com

# TABLE OF CONTENTS

# BEFORE YOU START READING . . .

**WOULD YOU DO ME A FAVOR, PLEASE?** Think about something you are really good at and write it down here (unless this is someone else's book or a library book, in which case use a sticky note—in fact, if it is not your book, go ahead and get some sticky notes or paper to use—you will need more as you read):

_____

_____

_____

_____

_____

Now think of something that you feel you are not very good at (or maybe really stink at!) and write it down here (same thing applies—if it's not your book, don't write in it):

_____

_____

_____

_____

Now, look at what you wrote down on the first page. Think about that skill you're really good at—what are some things that you have done in order to become so good at it?

Be as specific as you can. Don't just say, "I just am." I want details! Why are you so good at _____ ?

_____

_____

_____

_____

_____

_____

_____

_____

_____

Now think about the thing you said you were lousy at—what are some specific reasons why you think you stink at this skill or activity?

_____

_____

_____

_____

_____

_____

_____

_____

Now do one last thing for me (maybe!): Look at the statements in the following chart. Do you agree or disagree with them? Write your response down somewhere else if (you got this already, right?) it's not your book.

| | AGREE OR DISAGREE? | WHY? |
|---|---|---|
| Everyone can learn to draw. | | |
| If you practice for long enough, anyone can play varsity sports. | | |
| We inherit our weaknesses (like poor math or reading skills) from our parents. | | |
| Everyone can learn new things, but some people are just born smarter at certain things than others. | | |
| Musical talent is something that you are born with. | | |

Before we get to the first chapter, we must discuss a little issue. The title of this book is not exactly 100% true . . . there are actually some things that you can't do (but that wouldn't make a very good book title, would it?). There are some things that no matter how hard you try— you will not be able to do—these are typically things that are limiting us due to one or more of our physical attributes. You may not be able to be a classical ballerina because you are too tall or too short, or perhaps your awful vision will not allow you to be to be an airline pilot, or you may want to be a horse jockey but you grow to be more than 6 feet tall!

There are other things you might not be able to do, no matter how hard you work and practice—like being a famous athlete, singer, actress, or basically a famous anything! Why? Because so many people are trying to be famous at the same time. It is sometimes hard to stand out in a crowd where everyone else is trying to stand out. But that doesn't mean you shouldn't try!

Here is the important part to remember: Even though it might be very difficult to achieve something, that doesn't mean that you shouldn't enjoy the process of working toward your goals. Maybe you will never be a super famous singer, but that doesn't mean you can't work on your singing skills and have fun singing in a choir or starting a band or auditioning for your

school musical. Maybe you don't have good enough vision to be an airline pilot, but you love learning everything you can about airplanes—that passion you have might influence what you want to study in college, which may help you engineer a new kind of aircraft one day.

Finally, there are things that you may not be able to do because you have not learned what you need to know or the tools or strategies needed to do them yet. This book will help you figure out ways to do just that.

Okay, now we are ready to get into this book—which will help you unlock your potential. Notice I didn't say, "reach your full potential." Think about it—that simply is impossible and a really dumb phrase. Why? Because potential is endless, limitless, infinite. No one can ever reach his or her full potential . . . we can keep going and going and going!

This book will help you reach your goals and remind you that you have the potential to improve and succeed— you just have to unlock the secret to doing it.

Do you know what that secret is? One word: *Mindset*.

CHAPTER
1

# WHAT ARE MINDSETS, AND WHY ARE THEY IMPORTANT?

## What Are Mindsets Exactly?

Have you ever caught yourself thinking any of the following?

- I stink at math.
- I will never make the travel team.
- I am pretty good at art—I take after my mom.
- I have always been good at:

_____

_____ .

Why do you think those thoughts pop into our brains?

The way we think about things depends on our mindset. What is a "mindset"?

According to Merriam Webster (of dictionary fame, you know, the giant book you've seen in the library or your classroom that no one uses anymore because we have Google) the definition of a mindset is: "a particular way of thinking; a person's attitude or set of opinions about something."

||||||||||||||||||||||||||||||||||||||||||||||||||||||||||||||||||||||||||||||||||||||||||||||||||||||||||||||||||||||||||

# THE DEFINITION OF A MINDSET IS:
"a particular way of thinking; a person's attitude or set of opinions about something."

---

## Why Are Mindsets Important?

Mindsets are important because the way we think about ourselves, our potential, and our abilities affects how successful we will be with something. For example, let's say there was a new law that required every person your age to learn to play the guitar. What would your first thought be?

Why do these thoughts matter?

Well, if you decide that it is going to be too hard and that you will not have success, then there is a good chance that will happen. If you believe that you can learn to play the guitar because you consider yourself a musical person, then there is also a good chance that it may not happen.

Why? Because both of these thought processes are "fixed" or part of what we call a *fixed mindset*.

A fixed mindset is when you believe that you can or cannot do something because of abilities that you were born with. A fixed mindset is the belief that your skills, intelligence, and talents are something within you that cannot change. Some popular fixed mindset thoughts are "I am terrible at math" or "I have always been good at video games."

Let's think about that again: If you have a fixed mindset about a skill, situation, or activity, then you believe that your abilities *cannot improve very much or change*, and because of your thinking, you may choose not to participate, not to learn, and just give up. (That's a scary thought—think about what you may be missing!)

But here's the truth: You don't have to morph into fixed mindset thinking in these kinds of situations because you *can* change your abilities. (Phew! Thank goodness for that!)

What we have learned from neuroscience (the study of the brain and nervous system) is that we can change our skills, talents, and intelligence.

Wait, what? We can change our intelligence?

Yes, we can change our intelligence. People who believe the scientific facts that we can become smarter, more athletic, more artistic, more creative, more any-thing—have something called a *growth mindset*.

A growth mindset is when you believe that you can get bet-ter at and achieve just about anything that you put your mind to. This means that you are willing to put in the time, the perseverance, and the effort to do it.

Did you know that we control about 75% of our skills and achievement? That is a lot! So let's say that you don't think the 25% of your brain is very strong in math, or science, or learn-ing a foreign language, or whatever you wrote on page 2. You can still develop skills and talents in that area; you can even become an expert in that area—if you are willing to get more informa-tion about how to do it and stick with it.

Let's say that English is not your first language—you were born in a non-English-speaking country and no one at home speaks English in everyday conversation. On the first day of school you realize that you don't understand much of what the teacher is saying. You decide to apply growth mindset thinking to this situation—you will ask questions when you don't understand, practice speaking English as much as possible, ask for help when you need it, find online games that will help with English words, and ask someone at home to learn English with you. In other words, you will work, practice, and persevere—you are determined to learn English!

Now let's apply fixed mindset thinking to the same situation. You feel frustrated because you can't understand English. You think things like, "I will never catch up to everyone else, what's the point?" or "I can't do this." You don't put in much effort or ask for help because you feel like it is hopeless. You decide not to try very hard because you don't think you will be successful.

Most of us have some areas in our lives where we have a fixed mindset.

This does not mean that you can't actually do these things—
it just means that you may not think you can do these things
because you don't have the skills or talents, OR you may not
want to learn how to do these things. Why? Well, maybe because
they don't interest you or you are not willing to put in the time
and energy required to learn them—but it is not because you
*can't* learn them . . . it is because you *choose not* to learn them.

## A Secret About Mindsets

Here is a secret that not a lot of people know: There really
isn't any such thing as a growth mindset person or a fixed mindset person. The mindsets come into play based on the situation
that you are in—you either believe that with perseverance,
some mistakes along the way, and the right set of strategies that you can achieve, or you believe that
you were not born
with the capac-
ity or ability
to achieve in
this particular
area.

I know that I could learn to speak Japanese . . . but am I willing to put the time and work into learning it?

JAPANESE

JAPAN 101

YOU CAN LEARN JAPANESE!

| *FIXED MINDSET* | *GROWTH MINDSET* |
|---|---|
| Skills, talents, athletic ability, music/art ability, and intelligence are things we are born with—hereditary or genetic—and even though we can all learn new things, we will never be good at some things because we were not born with that talent, and the things that we are good at happen because we are born with strengths in these areas (not!). | Skills, talents, athletic ability, music/art ability, and intelligence are things we can learn with perseverance, resiliency, work ethic, and the right set of strategies. |

I know—you might be scratching your head thinking, "Huh?" Our parents or other relatives might tell us things like, "You are just like me. I was always good at soccer" or "Good writers run in our family" or "I was never good in math either. Poor thing, you take after me" or "Your dad and I are not creative people—so I guess that's why you're not very creative."

I am not going to tell you not to listen to your parents or relatives . . . well . . . actually . . . in this case, *don't listen to your parents or relatives* because heredity or genetics only have a very small influence on what you can or cannot achieve. YOU are in control of what you can do—if you have the right mindset. The rest of the chapters in this book will give you all of the secrets you need to use a growth mindset.

What do you notice in this picture?

Look at the apples that have fallen. Where have they landed?

What does this have to do with a growth mindset?

Why are a few apples really far from the tree?

Have you ever heard the expression, "The apple doesn't fall far from the tree"? What do you think it means? Do you agree with this idiom? Why or why not?

My notes: _____

_____

_____

_____

_____

_____

_____

_____

_____

_____

_____

_____

_____

_____

# CHAPTER 2

# HOW CAN I "GET" A GROWTH MINDSET?

Have you ever heard people say things like "Dream big!" or "Follow your dreams"? (Chances are likely you have—you might even have one of these sayings on your favorite T-shirt or a poster in your room.)

Dreaming of becoming something or doing something is wonderful—but don't you want more than just to dream about it?

I dream of going to school at Hogwarts and becoming a wizard...

Use the space below and write down something that you dream of doing.

It is not enough just to dream about becoming something or doing something you love. In order to become or do what you wrote (or to become more athletic, more musical, more artistic, or more intelligent), you also have to develop these things in yourself:

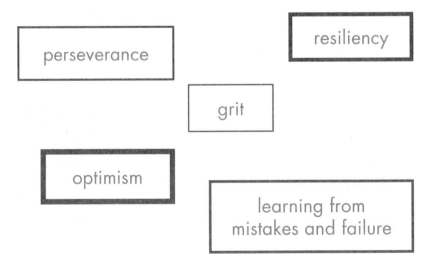

perseverance

resiliency

grit

optimism

learning from mistakes and failure

**ON A SIDE NOTE:**

Don't spend **ALL** of your time thinking about fulfilling your dreams and what you will do in the future. Enjoy and be happy about what is happening right now in your life! When we are happy, we can think more clearly and be more creative. Happiness can contribute to making us more productive people!

## Secret #1    The Glass Is Half Full

Let's first talk about optimism—a totally underrated but important thing that we should all practice. Optimism means that you try to see the best, or what is good, in every situation. The opposite of optimism is pessimism. Remember Eeyore, the donkey from Winnie the Pooh? Eeyore is NOT a good example of optimism. He sort of just shuffles along thinking about what is bad about the situation or the day. Some of us have "Eeyores" in our lives too—you might be friends with an Eeyore or you might even be related to one! Here is the tricky part about hanging out with a pessimistic person too much— it can be contagious! (No, not like a cold or flu or some other illness.) If we hang out with negative people all of the time . . .

we can actually begin to pick up on their negative thinking and start to become a pessimist as well!

If you already consider yourself a pessimist, you can change that—by simply practicing optimism.

Have you ever heard the expression "Is the glass half full or half empty?"

This is actually a good way to think about the difference between optimism and pessimism. If a glass is half full of water, can you still drink from it? (Yes!) Can the water still quench your thirst? (Yes!) An optimist will say the glass is half full because he or she sees what is good about it, but a pessimist will think that the glass is half empty because he or she focuses on what is missing rather than what is there.

Every day, there's likely to be stuff happening that can put you in a bad mood or make you mad. It happens to all of us. When this happens, catch yourself before you complain or start throwing shade at someone else and try to see the good in every situation. When you do this for a long period of time, your brain actually changes and optimistic thinking becomes easier!

Guess what? Practicing optimism is also practicing a growth mindset—optimistic people are people with hope, and we all want to feel hopeful.

## Secret #2  Remember These Growth Mindset Basics

In addition to developing optimism and the other things that are listed on page 20 (we'll get to those later), there are also some important things you must know in order to have a growth mindset:

— The brain is like a flexible piece of plastic—it has the ability to change and can get "smarter." This is a fact! Neuroscientists have proven that our brains are *malleable*. (Impress your friends with that word! It means your brain can change.) I'll share much more about the brain in Chapter 4 (if you are dying to know more about your brain and can't wait

two more chapters, just skip ahead—you're the one reading after all!).

— We need to recognize when we have a fixed mindset—those times when we say or think, "Ugh, I am terrible at that" or "I don't need to practice; I already know it."

— Realize that becoming good at something takes time, and some things take longer than others to be the best at . . . sometimes even years!

— The process or journey of accomplishing something is often more important than the outcome or what you have accomplished in the end. (Look at the cartoon above.)

— Mistakes and failures should be embraced—that is when we learn the most.

— Struggle is important. It builds our brains. If you never struggle, you probably are not being challenged enough. (More about this in Chapter 5.)

So, you can't really "get" a growth mindset—you have to practice having one. In other words, you need a growth mindset to utilize a growth mindset!

## ON A SIDE NOTE:

Here is a cool video that you may want to watch at some point: https://www.youtube.com/watch?v=qe4swkE_h6M*. It is called "Growth Mindset Changed His Life" (it is 2 minutes and 10 seconds long). It's about Lachie, a kid from Australia, and shows how he practiced and practiced and practiced and practiced and practiced (that's a lot of practicing!) on his skateboard until he could get to the top of a ramp, turn around, and come back down. He also shares his thoughts about having a growth mindset.

Use a smartphone or tablet to take a photo of this QR code—and others throughout this book—to be quickly directed to URLs.

Look back at what you wrote on page 20—that thing you dream about. What are some things that you can do now or in the future that might help that dream come true?

_____

_____

_____

_____

_____

If we want our dreams to come true, we need to make sure that we set goals and do the things we need to do to make them happen.

Another thing that contributes to growth mindset thinking is how people respond to us—what they say, how they praise us, and how they provide feedback to us . . . which is coming up next.

# THE POWER OF WORDS

Did you know that we can actually adjust the way we talk to each other (and the way we talk/think to ourselves) to help build growth mindset thinking? We should always focus on providing feedback and praise about what people DO, not who they are.

If someone tells you that you are really "smart," that might make you feel good and might make you

stand a little taller, for a little while—but the issue is what can happen later if people continually tell us that we are smart, brilliant, or a genius! (Parents and grandparents are good at this.) Eventually, you might start taking the easy way so that you always look smart. You may even avoid taking risks or avoid choosing challenging tasks, sports, classes, musical instruments, or video games and instead go the "safe" route where you know you will be successful and continue to look smart! (This is not a growth mindset idea!)

## Secret #3 Learn How to Talk to Your Friends

When we talk with our BFFs/squad/classmates, we should give them props about what they do. Consider saying things like:

- Hey, man, you really worked hard at that!
- Dude, that was awesome the way you stuck with it.
- That looked so hard, and you never gave up!
- I can tell you put a lot of time into that project—it is so cool!

When we "talk" with friends via social media we should also keep growth mindset talk in mind.

#goodeffort #keepitup #keeptrying
#persevere #donotgiveup #learnfrommistakes

Let's try a little quiz to see if you get what I mean (don't worry—this isn't like a quiz in school). Let's say a friend of yours just finished building the most spectacular LEGO structure ever—you have never seen anything like it in your life. I mean, it is awesome! What would you say to him or her?:

1.  You are the best LEGO builder I have ever seen!
2.  That must have taken you forever!
3.  You really worked hard on that!
4.  Your choice:

_____

_____

_____

_____

_____ !

If you picked the first one (*You are the best LEGO builder I have ever seen!*), then you've picked a fixed mindset statement. You are telling your friend that he or she is the best but not recognizing or praising the effort he or she put forth. Doesn't it sound like he or she was just born with the ability to create these awesome structures when you put it this way? (Which is impossible.)

If you picked the second one (*That must have taken you forever!*), then you are acknowledging that he or she put a lot of time into it—which does acknowledge his or her stick-to-it-iveness, but not really any effort. This is a growth mindset-ish response.

If you picked the third response (*You really worked hard on that!*), then you are letting him or her know that you realize that he or she put a lot of time, effort, and perseverance into the task. This is, of course, a growth mindset response.

If you wrote in something else, ask yourself these questions:

- Does your response praise who he or she is? (If it does, it is fixed.)
- Does your response praise what he or she actually did? (If it does, it is growth.)
- Does the response do neither? (This makes it neutral, neither fixed nor growth.)

If your response was not a growth mindset response, how could you change it to become one?

It takes practice to adjust the way we praise each other.

## Secret #4   Change How Others Praise You

I bet that you also have heard fixed mindset praise from others (just remember, they mean well). However, if you want to educate your friends and family (and even your teachers!) to use growth mindset praise, you may want to try thinking about how you respond to this praise. Think about these possible scenarios:

||||||||||||||||||||||||||||||||||||||||||||||||||||||||||||||||||||||||||||||||||||||||||||||||||||||||||||||||

**Dad:** You were the best on the field today! You scored the most points! (*fixed*)

**You:** Thanks, Dad, I have been practicing a lot, and I guess it showed. (*growth*)

---

||||||||||||||||||||||||||||||||||||||||||||||||||||||||||||||||||||||||||||||||||||||||||||||||||||||||||||||||

**BFF:** You are so lucky! You always do well on the math assessments! (*fixed*)

**You:** It's not luck—I ask the teacher to help me after school on things I don't understand yet and I always study. (*growth*)

---

||||||||||||||||||||||||||||||||||||||||||||||||||||||||||||||||||||||||||||||||||||||||||||||||||||||||||||||||

**Grandmother:** You are a natural-born writer! All of your stories are just perfect! (*fixed*)

**You:** Thanks, Granny, I do a lot of writing and work hard at it. (*growth*)

---

So, give it a try—start adjusting the praise that you give others by telling them how cool their hard work, effort, and perseverance is! Don't forget to respond to others in a way that shows growth mindset!

 **Don't Forget to Talk to Yourself (Really, It Works!)**

As you practice responding to others, you can also start adjusting the way you think or speak to yourself.

Changing from fixed to growth self-talk takes practice. Practice rephrasing the things you think or speak about yourself. Look at the phrases below and see how they can be adjusted to growth mindset statements.

| INSTEAD OF | SAY OR THINK |
|---|---|
| I give up! | I need to approach this a different way. |
| I am not smart enough to do this. | This may take time, but I will figure it out! |

Okay, get it? Now you try one:

| INSTEAD OF | SAY OR THINK |
|---|---|
| I am not good at this. | |

You can practice some more on page 112.

Here is another important piece of information: Mistakes, errors, and failures are all part of the learning process. If we never make mistakes, then we are not being challenged and not learning. So next time you say, "Ughhhh! I messed up again, I am so dumb!" instead say "Well that didn't work. I wonder what I should do differently next time?"

## Secret #6   The Power of Yet

One of the most important growth mindset words we can use is the word *yet*. Think about that word for a minute. Why do you think it is such an important word?

*Yet* is an optimistic word—it communicates that there is hope. It means that even if we can't do something right this minute, we will eventually.

In fact, we can add the word *yet* onto the end of just about any statement that begins with *I can't* . . .

➥ I can't do this . . . yet.

➥ I can't under-stand this book . . . yet.

➥ I can't possibly learn this math concept . . . yet.

↦ I can't play well enough to make that team . . . yet.

↦ I can't play this piece on my instrument . . . yet.

↦ I can't tie my shoes . . . yet. (JK . . . I think you can tie your shoes by now, but think about all of the practice it took to learn how!)

Actually, there is really not much that we should say "I can't" about!

## Secret #7  Don't Worry About Labels

So, as you can see, words are powerful. There are some words that adults might think are okay, but they can actually backfire—one of those words is *gifted*.

You may be in a school where kids take a test and find out if they are "gifted," "gifted and talented," "GT," "talented and gifted," "TAG," whatever they call it! Or you may be a person who has heard things like, "You have a gift for art" or "You are a gifted athlete." Maybe you, yourself, are in a gifted program or you know people who are.

Here is what we all need to remember: Yes, there are some kids (and you may be one of them) who have a small part of their brain that can learn faster, can solve really challenging problems, etc. But, remember that MOST of your brain is what *you* control. *You* have the ability to work side-by-side with any other person your age—you might (or might not) have to work harder or longer, but you can do it! We should never think that just because we are not in a "gifted" program that we cannot achieve at the same level. In fact, we may even realize at some point that we are not challenged enough and that we need some of the same opportunities that the "gifted" kids get—this is when we need to *advocate* for ourselves.

I know this guy, Scott, and he is the perfect example of what I am talking about. He never did well on "gifted" tests—in fact people thought he had learning challenges, and he was put in a class for kids with learning challenges. One day he decided to remove himself from the class because he did not think it was challenging enough for him (yes, he discussed his decision with his parents first). By making this decision, he was *advocating* for himself. Advocating means that you speak or act for yourself in order to improve your life—in Scott's case, he knew that he could handle more challenging work. He demonstrated perseverance and resiliency. He did great in the more challenging classes, but he really wanted to be in the "gifted" class . . . the problem was that his test score for the gifted program did not make the "cut."

Some of you might be thinking that what Scott was trying to do was crazier than a dog in a peanut-butter factory. Why wouldn't he want a class that was easy for him with easier work? He would probably get better grades if he stayed out of the "gifted" class . . . and probably have less homework!

Scott didn't care how challenging it was; he was interested in learning more things and being with other kids who thought like him, and he was very motivated to work hard and have success.

On the other hand, some of you may be relating to what Scott wanted—maybe you feel like you are underchallenged and you could use more acceleration and enrichment, but you didn't do well on the "gifted" test either. If you feel this way, and you know that you have the perseverance and work ethic to do it, then you should advocate for yourself. Here are some ideas on how to do that:

- Get your facts ready: grades (yuck, we will talk about grades later), attendance, and maybe even a written advocacy statement from one of your teachers.
- Let the school leaders know that you don't care about being officially identified or labeled as "gifted"—you just would like to participate in the class so that your learning needs will be met.
- Communicate clearly how motivated you are to do well—let the school leaders know that you possess the work ethic, perseverance, and resiliency to be successful!
- If you are not getting anywhere, advocate for a trial period in a class. Maybe 6 weeks or one quarter. If you show growth, you should stay in the class.

If you attend a public school, then it is possible that your school must follow school district policies for these classes or programs. They may have a silly rule that says that only kids who have a certain test score can participate. What should you do now?

- Call or e-mail the superintendent!

- Speak at a school board meeting!

- Start a petition!

- Get other kids and parents involved!

- Ask the "important people" who are in charge of what you learn and how you learn to develop more challenging learning opportunities for kids not in "gifted" classes, but who still need enriched and accelerated teaching and learning.

- Request more challenging instruction and work (not more work) from your teachers.

Why shouldn't all of us get the teaching and learning that we need?

**Back to Scott's story:** He ended up being in the gifted class without officially being "gifted" (according to the test score) . . . and yet the same thing happened when he was applying to colleges! Ugh! His SAT (a test that high school kids take to get into some colleges) score was not high enough to go to the college that he wanted to go to and major in psychology.

So, he did a tricky but very well-planned out move—Scott happened to also be a very good singer, so he applied to the college as a music major and got in! Then, after he took a psychology course and did very well, he advocated for himself again and changed his major from music to psychology!

So there you have it: Here is a kid who didn't do that well on the "important" tests he needed (the "gifted" test and the SAT), but was able to advocate for himself and was motivated and persevered in order to get what he wanted in life! Scott is now an adult and often shares his story with teachers. He is a happy and successful college professor, author, speaker, and researcher. Guess what he researches? Intelligence and creativity! He is famous in his field! (His name is Scott Barry Kaufman in case you want to look him up, and he has demonstrated a growth mindset many times throughout his life.)

Then, there is my friend Michelle—she never "passed" the "gifted" test either. Michelle always worked hard, did well in school, and was a wonderful writer. She became very interested in attending a school with a program that was only offered in one middle school in her school district. The program was focused on communications and not only offered challenging classes in writing, but also classes in television and film production. She really wanted into that program! Problem was (you probably guessed it), she was not "officially" identified as "gifted."

Not only was Michelle very motivated to somehow get into this program, but she also had a teacher, Mr. Patrick, who knew Michelle had the potential to be very successful in the program. He talked to Michelle and her mom and told them that this program would be perfect for Michelle. Michelle agreed. Her score on the tests may not have said she was "gifted," but Michelle knew this program would give her the chance to do what she loves most—read and write. So, Michelle advocated for herself, and Mr. Patrick advocated for Michelle. She got accepted into the program! Yes!

She was so excited—she couldn't wait for school to start. Then something unexpected happened: Once she began her new program, Michelle felt unprepared. She felt like the students from "gifted" elementary school programs had an advantage in their new middle school classroom. She knew she had to work harder though, and not only did Michelle demonstrate a growth mindset, but her parents, teachers, and advocates also had a growth mindset. Michelle realized that she was meant to be there, too. It didn't matter what elementary school she went to. It didn't matter what test score she had. She was in the classroom, ready to learn, and willing to work hard. As soon as Michelle looked beyond the label of "gifted," she felt right at home and ready to keep writing.

Michelle ended up receiving a scholarship and attending Northwestern University (she even finished school a semester early). She then attended the London School of Economics for her master's degree. She has a job where she feels happy and successful. Probably one of the most amazing things that Michelle has done is to begin an organization called Autism Articulated. Autism Articulated is a place where parents, friends, and basically anyone affected by autism have a place to share stories about how autism has changed their lives. Michelle (Byamugisha) is the founder. The website is http://www.autismarticulated.com if you want to learn more.

There are lots of kids like Scott and Michelle who have a growth mindset and advocate for themselves!

## ON A SIDE NOTE:

Remember that labels like "gifted," "learning disabled," "ADHD," "ESL," "autism" . . . I could go on and on . . . do not define you. These labels are not you. Your actions decide what happens in your life—labels don't.

If you *are* officially "gifted," then you need to be aware that you may tend to have fixed mindset thinking—you might be afraid to make a mistake for fear that someone will think you don't belong in a gifted program. I know some kids who are in gifted programs, and they are so afraid of taking a risk because they just don't want to be wrong or fail at something! It is also important to understand that it is good when you struggle with something: That just means you are being challenged—it does NOT mean that you don't belong in the class or program that you are in! Applying growth mindset thinking is very important when you are facing challenging tasks.

Let's talk about the times that someone may have said to one of us that we have a "gift" in an area—"You are a gifted artist" or "You have a gift for dancing." Is it possible that we may have been born with a tendency (not a "gift") to learn something well? Yes, but no one is born just knowing how to do something— that "gift" is not really a gift.

If you create wonderful art or dance well, then that is because you have practiced and developed that skill. *You* have done this—no one handed it to you like a gift, and you do need to keep practicing in order to continue to improve and grow.

Okay, that was a lot of information so let's summarize this chapter:

- Praise effort, perseverance, and process.
- YET, YET, YET, YET, YET.
- Labels do not define you—you are in control of what you want to learn.

# WHY DO I NEED TO LEARN ABOUT MY BRAIN IN ORDER TO HAVE A GROWTH MINDSET?

Before we get into this chapter, write down everything you know about your brain in the space below (or on your sticky notes).

_____

_____

_____

_____

_____

Most people your age do not know a whole lot about the brain—other than things like "it helps you think" or "it is pink and squishy and looks like spaghetti." The fact is, if you understand just a few important facts and concepts about the brain, you will have a better understanding about how you can develop your talents, skills, and intelligence.

**ON A SIDE NOTE:**

The Smarter Every Day Backwards Brain Bicycle is a really cool video (about 8 minutes long) about this guy who tried to ride a bike that works by doing the opposite of what you usually do to ride a bike. It took a lot of practice to change his brain pathways, and it is a good example of neuroplasticity. It can be found here: https://www.youtube.com/watch?v=MFzDaBzBlL0*. (It's really funny, too!)

## Secret #8   Your Brain Can Change!

Ever hear of the word *neuroplasticity*? (Get ready to learn another big word to impress your friends with!) It can be broken down into two smaller words: *neuro* and *plasticity*. Neuro refers to the brain and plasticity refers to the "plastic" nature of our brains, or the ability for our brains to change based on what we do. Our brains *can* change and become "smarter" when they get good brain exercise by learning new things and through effective practice and deliberate effort.

Here is a very simple example of neuroplasticity. One day, you come home from school and you find out that all of your clothes, toys, and "stuff" have been put in different places. Your clothes have been neatly folded in your old toy box; your toys, video games, building materials, and crafting supplies are in your dresser drawers; and your socks are in a basket. For the first few days, you open a drawer to get clothes out and find something else—it takes several days for your brain to adjust to this new arrangement. Eventually, it does, and you automatically go to the toy box to get your clothes without even thinking much about it! Your brain was able to adjust to the new arrangement thanks to neuroplasticity.

The opposite can happen to your brain as well: It can become sluggish when it doesn't get much exercise, doesn't do much thinking, and is basically a couch potato. (Think about how some of your school skills slack off during the summer if you don't practice them.)

Some easy ways to give your brain a mini-workout include:

- Eat your next meal (or brush your teeth) with your non-dominant hand. Are you right-handed? Eat with your left hand. Are you left-handed? Eat with your right hand. Are you ambidextrous? Well, then, this activity will not provide a good brain workout for you!

- Go into the kitchen and pick up an object (a spatula, pan, potato masher, a plate, a bowl, anything!). Think of five other ways that the object could be used than its intended use.

- Sit at a different seat at the table when you have a meal or ask your mom or dad to shop at the grocery store the opposite way that you typically do. Your brain benefits from any kind of new experience.

 # Your Brain Can Get Smarter! And Stronger!

So how exactly do our brains become smarter? Here is a simple way to understand what happens in our brains when we learn or experience something new:

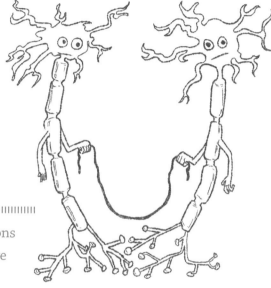

**Fact:** We have billions of brain cells; these are called *neurons*.

---

**Fact:** When we learn something new, neurons begin to form weak connections between each other. (Imagine a skinny piece of thread connecting a few neurons.)

---

**Fact:** The more you understand and practice that new thing, the stronger the connection gets. (Imagine a thick, strong piece of rope connecting the neurons.)

---

**Fact:** The more neural connections, the smarter you are!

So when you are facing a challenging task, visualize (make a picture in your head) your neurons trying to connect.

Here is a fact that not too many people know: When we struggle, or something seems too hard, that is actually awesome for your brain! That means that your neurons need to work hard to connect, which is a great brain workout. This tough workout will make you smarter.

When we struggle and something is too hard for us—do you know what most of us do? Go on . . . guess . . . please? Just guess, and write your guess here:

_____

_____

_____

If you wrote that we give up or quit, then you are right—there are times when things seem so incredibly difficult that we just give up.

Instead of giving up, you need to be challenged and learn new things so that new neural connections are made in your brain.

On the next page, you will see an outline of a brain. Draw this on a separate piece of paper if this is not your book.

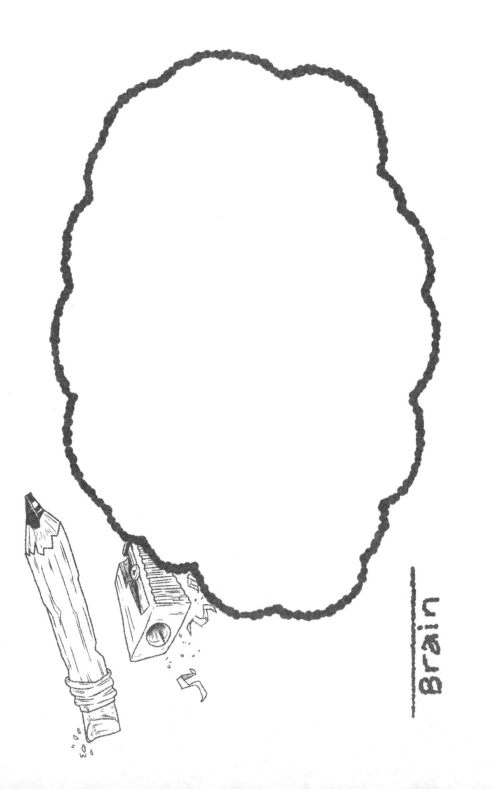

Brain

- To begin, draw about eight small neurons (they don't have to look exactly like a neuron).
- Think of something that you understand really well, like multiplication, or punctuation, collaboration, discombobulation (OK, I am getting carried away), or illustration, modernization, orchestration, recontamination (Stop? I can't stop!), or refrigeration, reinfestation, synchronization (really, it's fun!), or telecommunication, vaporization, or (you really want me to stop now?). OK, well, think of anything that you can do well or know well, and draw a thick line between two neurons to show that you know this well—label the connection for the thing you know well.
- Think of something that you know or can do, but maybe not perfectly well yet . . . maybe something like swimming or dribbling a basketball or writing a persuasive paper—something that you still need to practice. Draw a thinner line between two neurons and label this with skill that you are working on.

- Now think of something that you are just beginning to learn—maybe something in math like finding the area of a triangle, quadrilateral, and/or polygon. Use a dashed line like - - - - - - - to represent this brand-new learning.

What will happen to this weak connection when you practice this skill? Yep, it will get thicker and stronger! What happens to a strong connection if you stop using this knowledge? Yep, it gets weaker and sometimes even disconnects from other neurons. We will forget things if we don't review them and practice.

Our brains are malleable (remember that word?); they change all of the time. Neurons form new connections as we learn and connections weaken when we don't use them. Scientists have done lots of research on the plasticity of the brain. In fact, scientists have learned that even the brains of rats become smarter when they practice a new skill. (Some develop great problem-solving skills going through a maze!)

A lot of times we think that we are trying as hard as we can, but we actually are not—so our brains are not really getting a good workout. Our parents and teachers remind us to put forth "effort"—and we think we are—but what does it actually mean to put forth effort? Here are some things that we need to do in order to really put forth effort:

- Really concentrate on what you are working on. Turn off the TV and put your phone away when you are learning something new; it is not the time to multitask.

- Be willing to put the time into *learning* (not just finishing) what you are working on.
- Persevere—if the strategy that you are using is not working, try something else.
- Have determination. Be committed to learning and doing it well.
- Use any feedback that anyone has given you to learn and complete the task. Feedback may come from coaches, music and art instructors, teachers, parents, and maybe even a website or a writing program.
- Know *when* and *who* to ask for help and know how to ask for it. Be specific . . . don't just say "I don't get this."

This will all lead to what is called *effective effort*. By practicing effective effort, not only do our brains get a good workout, but it also gives us the power to be successful . . . and you know what else? When we put forth effective effort, it shows that we care about what we are doing.

OK, you might be thinking, but does it really work?

Research was done with middle school kids in New York City: half of the kids were taught about growth mindset and the other half were not. All of the kids were in the same math group and had about the same grades. The kids who learned

about growth mindset showed improvement in math over a 2-year period. One of the things that many of the students reported is that they visualized their neurons connecting any time they really got stuck and wanted to give up. They knew that if they continued to put forth effective effort and tried a variety of ways to understand, they would get those neurons to connect and become smarter in math!

So, next time you feel stuck, like you're not getting the hang of something, or that your brain hurts from thinking so hard, just picture those neurons getting to work in your brain. Every

neural connection that is made makes your brain "denser." The denser the brain, the smarter you get!

Our brains need to be in great shape to learn. Think about how we feel if we don't sleep well one night or go to bed too late . . . not only are our bodies tired, but our brains feel foggy and our thoughts are murky. We have to take care of our brains, too!

Now think about the question that is the title of this chapter, "Why do I need to learn about my brain in order to have a growth mindset?" Jot down some thoughts here:

_____

_____

_____

_____

_____

_____

_____

_____

_____

Compare your thoughts to the those found on p. 116 in the Extras section.

# WHY CAN'T I QUIT WHEN THINGS GET HARD?

What comes to mind when you see or hear the word *perseverance*? I have certainly mentioned it more than a few times in this book so far. Remember the stories of *The Little Engine That Could* or the *Tortoise and the Hare*? Both stories demonstrate perseverance. The Little Engine tries to make his way up that very steep hill and does not give up until he is successful, and it is the tortoise that demonstrates perseverance as he slowly "races" the hare (. . . and why can't they just be called a turtle and rabbit?).

Two of the most important things that we can develop in ourselves are perseverance and resiliency.

|||||||||||||||||||||||||||||||||||||||||||||||||||||||||||||||||||||||||||||||||||||||||||||||||||||

**Perseverance:** Putting forth effort to understand or get something done

**Resiliency:** To bounce back from any obstacle or setback

---

## Secret #10 Bounce Back From Setbacks

We all know that a lot of annoying things pop up in life. Usually, however, they are temporary bumps in the road—things like the computer crashing, getting injured, forgetting a book you need for school, everything being due on the same day, getting picked on, or a friend or family member being sick. How we handle these kinds of situations depends on how resilient we are.

Some of us stay calm when we face things that are frustrating or difficult. Even if we handle difficulties calmly and demonstrate

resilience, it doesn't mean that we still don't worry about them. It's okay to worry sometimes. Some of us get stressed or anxious or freak out. Some of just can't stand it when we are being corrected by someone (that used to be me) and struggle to just consider it feedback (remember, feedback helps us improve!). It *can* be annoying when we are corrected—especially when it is done in a harsh or public way. In this case, very kindly, professionally, and respectfully ask the person who has corrected you in a harsh or public way to provide the feedback privately if possible and to provide it in a respectful way. By the way, sometimes we also provide unsolicited (uninvited) feedback to our friends. You need to be careful because sometimes that feedback can feel like criticism to your friend—even if that is not your intention. Be sure to communicate with your friends to make sure that they actually want feedback for the particular situation that they are in.

How we handle challenges in our life has to do with our resilience. Being resilient means that we have the ability to bounce back (instead of giving up) after a setback.

So, what can we do to help build our resiliency? Here are a few secrets for bouncing back:

- *Really understand what it means to be resilient.* When you are persevering to learn something new or accomplish a task and you fail or something gets in the way of the learning, can you bounce back and keep going? Resiliency is not just correcting an error or redoing something. Resiliency is overcoming barriers that get in your way.
- *Take care of yourself.* You may have heard the message to "think about others first"—and of course it is very important to be kind and helpful to others—but in order to build resiliency, we must take care of *our* bodies and *our* minds first so that we can help ourselves and help others. There are a few important things you can do because they can really help stressful situations and therefore can contribute to resiliency, including:
  - ⟳ Get a good night's sleep and eat healthy food. Foods that really help our brain include eggs, fish, nuts, bananas, and berries (blueberries, strawberries, raspberries, and blackberries).
  - ⟳ Balance busy time with "downtime" (relax, read, listen to music, talk with family or friends) and fun time.

- *Practice flexibility.* Change is a part of life. When you expect some things to go one way and they ended up going another, just shrug it off and go with the flow.

- *Be friendly.* Make lots of friends and see what is good in people. Friends can sometimes help us through challenging times, and we can do the same for them.
- *Practice optimism.* When life gives us challenges, try to see the good in every situation—the more optimistic we are, the better we will be able to handle those challenges. Seeing the funny parts of life also helps us practice optimism.
- *Turn to a higher power.* If you or your family have religious beliefs, those beliefs can contribute to your level of resiliency. Pray, attend a service, or talk with a minister, priest, rabbi, mullah, or any clergy about the challenge you are facing. Turning to your religious beliefs can be particularly helpful when someone you love is sick or has passed away.
- *Set goals.* If you are trying to learn something new and obstacles keep popping up, then set some small goals along the way to help you accomplish the task. (More on goal-setting in Chapter 7.)
- *Watch out for information on the Internet.* Sometimes when we face a challenge we want to get more information about it, so we jump right on the Internet to learn more. But some of the websites that we get information from are not very accurate and can cause more worry and make things feel hopeless.
- *Meditate.* Yep, you heard me right—meditation can help us manage the stress and worry we may have. It can help us stay calm, which helps us be resilient. The website, Cosmic Kids (http://www.cosmickids.com) has

some cool meditation videos. You can also try the DreamyKid Meditation App.

— *Reflect on the situation.* Probably one of the most important things that we need to do when we face obstacles and challenging situations is to learn to reflect. I know, you might be thinking, what on Earth does that mean? Well, keep reading!

## Secret #11  Reflect on What Went Wrong

Reflecting means to take some time (a few minutes to a few days or more) and really think about what went wrong, what went well, and how you might change the way that you are approaching the learning. Begin making it a habit to reflect and pay close attention to your thoughts—talk yourself out of that fixed mindset that might be sneaking in.

Reflecting on our learning or process is important. You can reflect silently or out loud (it depends on where you are).

You may be wondering if I'm asking you to talk to yourself

The next time I have a paper due, I will take the time to really proofread it carefully and double-check the rubric to make sure that I have included everything that is required.

by reflecting out loud—yes, actually, you should! Thinking out loud can help you tremendously to solve and get past obstacles. For example, this girl I know, Bella, was trying to put together one of those tall, skinny bookshelves that come in lots of pieces—no tools were required and the directions did not have words, just pictures. She studied the pictures, then got to it and began screwing these tube-like pole thingies into flat shelves. She was almost done when she stopped and reflected aloud, "Wait, if I keep doing it this way, how will the last shelf be attached?" She paused and really studied what she had built and looked at the pictures on the directions again. She said, "If I take it completely apart and start from the top, instead of the bottom, I think it may work." So she took it apart and began building again. It worked . . . sort of . . . but she then realized that she wanted to add an additional shelf to the top. "I think I am going to have to take it apart again and start over," she said. Then she paused and really thought about it harder. "Wait, I can add this one to the bottom because it has an area to attach the feet to." Which is what she did . . . and ta-da! Her bookshelf was complete!

Bella's ability to reflect on her process, recognize her mistake, persevere by starting over, reflect again, and solve the problem were all part of her resiliency. She could have just given up the first time she realized that she made a mistake—she could have said "I can't do this" and asked her mom to do it. Instead, Bella showed that she was resilient.

To practice reflecting, you may want to use these sentence starters and questions:

- I wonder why . . . ?
- Maybe I could have approached this in a different way.

- I am surprised that . . .
- Do I understand how this connects to something that I already understand?
- What should I do next?
- Maybe I could try doing it this way.

## Secret #12 Struggle, Struggle, Struggle

Here is a secret that not too many people know: You canNOT develop resiliency in school if you are underchallenged.

What do you think it means to be under-challenged? (Stop here and think about that for a minute.)

When we are under-challenged, things come easily for us. We understand what is being taught, we do well on assignments, and sometimes even spend too much time on concepts that we understood 3 days ago! Being underchallenged means we don't struggle as much as we need to when learning something new. You may think that is a good thing, but it's not—we need to give our brain a good workout every day. Struggling helps us do that. Struggle also lets us know that we are really learning something new.

Ever hear of the phrase *productive struggle*? (Wait, what? How can struggling be productive?) During productive struggle, you can wrestle with tasks, try a bunch of different strategies, and eventually understand or have success with something. When you are struggling with something, it is okay to get some guidance from parents, teachers, or coaches, just don't let them overhelp! Parents and teachers sometimes think it is easier to swoop in and just do something for you. Let them know that even though it may take a little longer, you want to try to do it yourself.

Another way to struggle productively is by playing games that become more challenging as they go. Games like *Rush Hour* or *Chocolate Fix* (the company Thinkfun makes these) are great to play to experience increasing challenges (you can play the actual games or download the free apps). *Portal 2* is a video game that does the same thing—as levels get harder, it strengthens the neural connections in our brain.

You must struggle to build resiliency (I know, I already said that—but it is worth saying again).

Some of us do a good job of practicing strong resiliency outside of school. You might have a situation at home that requires you to be strong and resilient, or you may practice resiliency during sports or other afterschool activities. Then, when it comes to school, well . . . now that's a different story. As soon as things get tough at school, you can get frustrated. That is when you need to practice reflecting on how you are approaching the task and what you might need to do differently in order to have success.

One of the things that many of us do is that we just want to get things done, and we are so focused on being done that we forget to actually learn along

the way! Completing an assignment and actually learning are not the same thing.

Think about some of your favorite books. Are any of the characters resilient? Do they persevere when things get tough? Here are some of my favorite books that have characters who demonstrate perseverance and resiliency.

| BOOK TITLE AND AUTHOR | CHARACTER | SOMETHING TO THINK ABOUT |
|---|---|---|
| *Wonder* by R. J. Palacio | Auggie | Auggie (who has a facial deformity) was starting school for the first time in grade 5. Think about some of the things he had to do to be resilient while he was adjusting. |
| *Out of My Mind* by Sharon Draper | Melody | Think about some of the obstacles that Melody has had to overcome due to her disability. |

| BOOK TITLE AND AUTHOR | CHARACTER | SOMETHING TO THINK ABOUT |
| --- | --- | --- |
| *A Long Walk to Water* by Linda Sue Park | Salva | Think about all of the challenges that Salva faced as he tried to make his way through the desert. |
| ANY Harry Potter book by J. K. Rowling | Harry | Okay, where to begin? Here are a few of the things that Harry demonstrated perseverance and resiliency against: trolls, dragons, devil's snare, the Whomping Willow, the basilisk, the grindylow, dementors, and, of course, He Who Must Not Be Named! Not to mention the perseverance and resiliency he demonstrated during the whole Triwizard Tournament! Think about all of the strategies that Harry used to get through these tough situations. |
| *Unstoppable* by Tim Green | Harrison | Think about Harrison's resilience while in foster care—and then his perseverance learning to play football and learning to be a team player. How did he apply those same perseverance skills when he was facing health challenges? |
| *Amina's Voice* by Hena Kahn | Amina | Think about how Amina struggled to prepare for the competition. She didn't care about winning, she just did not want to feel embarrassed. |

What books and characters would you add?

_____

_____

_____

_____

_____

## Secret #13  Get Gritty

Every hear of the word *grit*? I like to think of grit as per-severance with some caffeinated soft drinks thrown in. Grit means to stick with something over a long period of time. So what is a long period of time? Did you ever see a little kid try to learn to ride a bike or tie his shoes? (A long period of time for a 4-year-old might be 30 minutes!)

Here's the thing, I don't find myself having grit about something that I am not very interested in. If you are going to spend years learning how to play a musical instrument, then it is important to have some kind of interest or passion in that instrument. From our interests, passion grows. When we per-severe and are passionate about something, we tend to have more "grit."

So, what happens if we really are not very interested in what we are being taught? How can we stay motivated enough to put forth effort and to work hard? Well, one thing we can do is to really understand what the purpose of the learning is. Why on Earth do we have to learn this?

If we have an understanding about why it is important, then we are more likely to be committed to working hard on it. If your teacher, parent, or coach has not shared the reason or purpose for what you are learning . . . just ask! But ask in a respectful way . . . NOT in a whiny voice saying, "Why do we have to do this?" Instead, ask in a way that will not be misinterpreted as disrespectful; something like:

- I think I could get the hang of this if I understood why it's important to learn this.

  *or*

- I am having trouble sticking with this. Could you tell me what the purpose of learning this is? I think it would help me.

  *or*

- Can you help me connect this to something that I already know or something we have already learned?

Interests also influence when and if we should quit something. It is okay to quit some things that are our choice and we are not that interested in, but we have to make sure we are quitting for the right reasons and at the right time. We don't want to quit halfway through taking a class, once a sports season has already started, or after making a commitment to be a mother's helper or rake a neighbor's leaves. We don't want to quit after a frustrating or hard day.

Interested in one way to find out how "gritty" you are? There is a Grit Scale that has eight questions for you to answer in order to get an idea of how gritty you are.

If you want to print the questions, use this website: http://www.sjdm.org/dmidi/files/Grit-8-item.pdf. If you want to answer the questions online, use this website: http://www.souldirected.com/survey_shortgritscale.php.

We have talked about resiliency, perseverance, and grit. Think about what they mean to you and create emojis that represent each one.

**What would an emoji for resiliency look like?**

**What would an emoji for perseverance look like?**

What would an emoji for grit look like?

# WAIT, WHAT?
# I CAN LEARN
# FROM FAILURE?

We've talked about perseverance, resilience, and grit, but even when all of those are in place, we still make mistakes and fail. This is great, because our brains absolutely love it when we mess something up. Does that sound crazy? Maybe . . . but, remember, our brains are happy when they are having a good workout!

## Secret #14 Don't Be Afraid of Mistakes

When you make a mistake and really think about what went wrong (or reflect on it), this is a valuable process. Think about a time when you got an assignment back from a teacher and you didn't do as well as you expected to do. If you are like most kids, then you probably just look at the score or grade and stuff it in your desk, locker, or backpack.

What you need to do is reflect on it—make sure that you read any teacher comments that are written, make sure you understand what the teacher is saying, and look at the errors. Consider the error as data—something to learn from. Sometimes you make errors just because you didn't read the directions well or because the directions were confusing. If the teacher did not write any comments and you can't figure out where your error was, just ask your teacher! Say or e-mail something like this: "I really don't want to make these same mistakes again; can you please show me what I did not understand?" Some schools even have new web-based programs that provide us with feedback on our writing process—basically the computer will provide feedback like "Revise your word choice in your introduction." (Incredible what computers can do these days!)

It doesn't matter if you get the feedback in the form of comments written on the assignment, from a web-based program, or right from your coach, teacher, or parent's mouth—feedback is what helps us improve our understanding of things. Failure is a type of feedback—feedback you grow from. Never be afraid to start over.

You can't be afraid of making mistakes and failing at something. We all (kids and adults) need to get out of our comfort zone. What does that mean, you ask? It means that you should take advantage of opportunities to try new things that you might think you can't do. It can be simple things like trying new foods, hanging out with new friends, playing a new sport, or starting a new hobby. Read a book that you typically would not chose. Watch TV shows that you usually ignore. Download an app that is different from what you usually do.

### ON A SIDE NOTE:

There is a video that shows what can happen when a first grader uses feedback from the other kids in his class to improve his work. It is called "Austin's Butterfly" (approximately 6 minutes long). It is actually a video for teachers, but it is also helpful for kids to watch. It is amazing to see the difference between Austin's first attempt and his final draft! You can find it at: https://vimeo.com/38247060*.

Be comfortable with being uncomfortable. Try not to wiggle out of situations that make you uncomfortable because you are not good at something or you don't know much about it.

Try something new every day (okay, how about at least once a week?).

## Secret #15 Remember That Greatness Can Come From Failure

Many things that we use every day of our lives were invented because a mistake was made or another invention failed. Errors and failures can sometimes work out even better than the intended goal! Did you know these things were originally thought of as failures?

— *Post-it Notes.* Inventing sticky notes was not the intention of chemist Spencer Silver, who worked for the 3M company. He was actually trying to invent a megastrong glue, but made a mistake and invented a superweak one instead. Thus, Post-it Notes were born!

— *Play-Doh.* (Don't you love the smell of Play-Doh?) It was accidentally invented by inventors Joseph McVicker and Noah McVicker—they were trying to create wallpaper cleaner! A year later, in 1956, it was sold by a toy company and called Play-Doh.

— *Silly Putty.* An engineer named James Wright tried to create an inexpensive substitute for synthetic rubber, but he made a big mistake when he accidentally dropped boric acid into an oil mixture. The result was a stretchy, bouncy substance that was eventually sold as a toy.

— *Chocolate chip cookies.* In 1937, Ruth Wakefield was making butter cookies and thought she would make them all chocolate instead. She cut a bar of chocolate into tiny pieces and added them to the cookie dough. She thought that the chocolate would melt completely and she would have chocolate cookies. When the cookies came out of the oven, the chocolate hadn't melted at all! Instead, the "chocolate chips" had kept their form.

- *Potato chips.* One day in 1853 at a diner in New York, George Crum made French fries for a customer. The customer complained that the fries were too thick. Crum made a new batch of fries that were very, very thin—he wanted to annoy the picky customer. Well, the customer loved them, and potato chips were invented.
- *Popsicles.* In 1905, Frank Epperson mixed up a common fruit-flavored soda drink out of powder and water. He accidentally left it outside overnight on a cold night, with the stirring stick still in the cup. In the morning, the drink had frozen around the stick. He popped it out of the cup and licked it—a popsicle!

For years I have heard people say, "We learn from our mistakes." I never really understood what that meant until I learned more about having a growth mindset. You only learn from mistakes if you take the opportunity to do just that!

There are also a lot of "famous" people who made lot of mistakes and failed lots of times before they had success:

- *Michael Jordan*, the famous basketball player, didn't make his high school team when he tried out as a sophomore. He used failure to motivate him to prac-  tice. Check out this cool commercial where he talks about all of his failures: https://www.youtube.com/ watch?v=45mMioJ5szc *.
- *Rihanna*, the famous singer, has had a lot of difficulties in her life. Her childhood was challenging because her

dad was addicted to drugs. She could have given up, but instead her motto in life is, "Never a failure, always a lesson."

— *J. K. Rowling*, author of all of the Harry Potter books, was rejected by 12 other publishers before she was finally able to get the first Harry Potter book published. She wrote it when she was a single mom who was on welfare. She said in an interview, "It is impossible to live without failing at something."

— Ever hear of the *Wright Brothers*? Orville and Wilbur Wright are known as one of the first inventors of the airplane. They built seven flying machines, and they all crashed! They learned from each mistake along the way.

— *Jack Andraka* was a 15-year-old student when he came up with an idea that he wanted to try. He wanted to create a medical test that would help detect pancreatic cancer. He wrote to research labs all over the country—199 of them rejected him and said that he could not use their labs to work on his idea. The 200th lab at Johns Hopkins University accepted him. There, Jack successfully developed a pancreatic cancer test that is much better and less expensive than anything that was used before. He was still in high school when he accomplished this!

Be curious about your errors or lack of success. Reflect about why the mistake occurred. Be sure to experiment, create, struggle, persist, try new things, and know that failure is all part of the learning process.

# CHAPTER 7

# WHY SHOULD I SET GOALS FOR MYSELF?

Have you ever set a goal for yourself? You know, things like "My goal is to get an A+ in science," or "I am going to make the team this year," or "I am not going to fight with my brother"?

Setting goals is an important part of having a growth mindset. Goal-setting is something that you will do your entire life! You will not necessarily write them down (although that is not a bad idea), but you should have your goals in mind. They could be very general, long-term goals like going to college or traveling or eating healthy. They could also be very specific goals. Let's look at what kind of goals will help you apply growth mindset thinking.

## Secret #16  Write Active, Strategic Goals for Yourself

Think about some things that you would like to achieve—one for school, one for home, and one for a hobby or sport that you participate in. Write them below.

**A goal for school:** _____

_____

_____

**A goal for home:** _____

_____

_____

**A goal for an activity, hobby, sport, or something in the arts:**

_____

_____

_____

Now think about how you are going to get there:

**In order to reach my goal for school, I will:**

_____

_____

_____ .

**In order to reach my goal for home, I will:**

_____

_____

_____ .

**In order to reach my goal for my activity, I will:**

_____

_____

_____ .

What you just wrote above should actually be your goals! These are the *actions* or *strategies* that you will use to help meet your goal. Let's look at the three goals that I used for an example.

**A goal for school:** *My goal is to get an A+ in science.*

**In order to reach my goal for school, I will:** *ask more questions during science class when I do not really understand something.*

Let's think about that for a minute—could asking more questions in science class in order to help you understand what you are learning improve your grade? Yes! Your goals need to be focused on an action, strategy, or process.

Here is another one:

**A goal for home:** *I am not going to fight with my brother.*

**In order to reach my goal for home, I will:** *walk away from situations that could lead to fighting with my brother.*

Will walking away from your brother help you not fight with him? It could help a little, unless your brother follows you! What other strategy could you use? Here are some ideas:
- I will not react when he makes me mad.
- I will try to stay out of his business.
- I will not be mean to my brother.
- When he picks on me, I will say something nice to him. (This might be a challenging one.)

Remember, one or more of these strategies should actually be your goal!

**A goal for an activity:** *I am going to make the soccer team this year.*

**In order to reach my goal for this sport, I will:** *practice my weakest skills, passing and scoring, every day.*

(Notice that the example doesn't just say, "I will practice every day." In order to make the team, you need to practice the skills that you are not very good at yet.)

Here are some more to try (I did the first two to get you started):

| INSTEAD OF THESE GOALS . . . | TRY THESE . . . |
|---|---|
| I will get an A in social studies. | *I will to learn how to take helpful notes in class.* |
| I will pass all of my math tests. | *I will review new math concepts at home as soon as they are taught.* |

| INSTEAD OF THESE GOALS... | TRY THESE... |
|---|---|
| I will make the basketball team. | |
| I will be first-chair flute in band. | |
| I will learn how to speak sign language. | |
| I will get a solo in the school chorus. | |

What is important in goal-setting is that we chose goals that focus on the journey instead of the end, just like the examples I just gave you and the ones you just came up with.

## Secret #17　Practice Deliberately

In order to reach some goals we must do something called *deliberate practice*. Not just regular old practice, but effective, deliberate practice. This is a specific kind of practice that is very planned and purposeful. The planning and purpose is focused on improving performance. It is not about just repeating something over and over without really thinking about it . . . you need to be very focused on what you are practicing and why you are practicing.

In the 1950s, there was a famous golfer named Ben Hogan—he is a great example of what effective, deliberate practice is because he loved to practice golf! He would be at the practice tee as soon as the sun came up, and he hit golf balls for most of the day. Every time he practiced, he worked on a specific skill to improve his swing. Many say that he became a champion because he practiced for 12 hours a day!

Ever hear of the famous tennis players Venus Williams and Serena Williams? They have participated in deliberate tennis practice since they were 7 and 8 years old! They would get up by 6 a.m. and practice tennis each day before going to school. They wouldn't just go and practice casually either; they worked on specific skills to improve their game.

The famous composer Mozart had something interesting to say about practicing:

> It is a mistake to think that the practice of my art has become easy to me. I assure you, dear friend, no one has given so much care to the study of composition as I. There is scarcely a famous master in music whose works I have not frequently and diligently studied.

What do you think Mozart means when he says, "no one has given so much care to the study of composition as I" (when he says "composition," he is referring to writing music)?

What about, "There is scarcely a famous master in music whose works I have not frequently and diligently studied"?

He is referring to the fact that he has had success because not only does he practice, but also spends a lot of time looking through, playing, and studying the music of other famous composers.

Here are some suggestions for effective practice:

Choose a location where all of the materials that you will need are close by.

Establish a regular routine and time for practice.

Have fun! Use creative strategies to practice.

Make sure that your practice is focused on a specific skill.

Consider writing down or using an app to track progress over time.

Focus on hard work and effort—not perfection.

Take breaks when you need to refocus and recharge your energy.

## Secret #18 Set Growth Mindset Goals

If you are not sure what kind of goals you want to work toward, start with growth mindset goals. These are goals that will actually help you apply growth mindset thinking to lots of different situations!

Here are some examples of growth mindset goals:

- I will have high expectations of myself.
- I will approach things in a new way if I am not having success.
- I will ask for more challenging work if the work I am given does not require much effort.
- I will work longer at trying to figure something out and will not give up quickly.
- I will ask questions when I do not understand something.
- I will review all of my work and modify or redo it to improve.
- I will no longer say or think, "I can't do this," or "This is too hard."
- In school, I will request time after class to work with my teacher or a study buddy to make sure that I understand.
- I will not be disappointed when I fail or make a mistake. Instead, I will figure out what I need to do differently the next time.

## Secret #19 Use Lots of Strategies to Reach Your Goals

Sometimes it is good to have several strategies as goals to reach a bigger goal. Here is a simple example using Pokémon Go. My goal was to reach Level 30 in Pokémon Go. Sounded like a reasonable goal, until I realized how many points were required to reach each level. (Did you know that it takes 350,000 XP just to get from level 29 to 30?) Here is another thing you should know—I collect the Pokémon, but I don't use the gyms, I don't participate in raid battles, and I don't spend any money buying extra things in the Pokémon Go store. (I know some of you might think that is weird, but that's what I enjoy.) So I collect them, transfer them, evolve them, hatch eggs, and find lots of Pokéstops.

If I want to reach Level 30, what are some of the strategies that I should consider? It would make the most sense to use many of these strategies if I want to get to Level 30 within the next year or two (I consider this a long-term goal!):

- Use a Lucky Egg when I am ready to evolve many Pokémon during the 30 minutes before the egg expires.
- Hang out at a park or somewhere else that has a lot of Pokémon and Pokéstops. (I happen to live in a Pokémon desert!)
- Never break a 7-day streak for Pokéstops or Pokémon.
- Discard extra Potions and Revive so that I can store more Poké Balls and Razz, Nanab, and Pinap berries.

What other strategies could you add? If you go to gyms and participate in raid battles, you are sure to have more strategies!

Here is another example that some of you may be able to relate to. Think about this: How did Harry Potter learn to be such a great Quidditch player? He never even heard of Quidditch before going to Hogwarts, so it's not like he had practiced his whole life.

Let's say Harry set a goal of not only making the Gryffindor Quidditch team, but also becoming a Seeker. He would need to use several strategies to reach that goal. Here are some of the strategies that he should consider:

- He should deliberately practice speed and precision on his broom while only holding on with one hand or no hands at all. (He needs his hands to catch the Golden Snitch.)
- He should practice reacting quickly when a Bludger is heading toward him.
- He should deliberately practice catching the Golden Snitch at different heights, speeds, and spots on the field.

Harry Potter would need to use all of these strategies to become a successful Seeker on the Gryffindor Quidditch team. What other strategies could you add?

So, go ahead, and set some goals. Remember goals should *not* be things like, "I will get an A or make honor roll or win a contest"—they should include an action or strategy for getting there. Good goal-setting really helps you apply growth mindset thinking!

CHAPTER
8

# NOW THAT YOU ARE A GROWTH MINDSET EXPERT . . .

Well, actually you are not a growth mindset expert—yet. It takes more than reading a book or talking about it in school to become an expert in growth mindset. It takes practice

to apply this kind of thinking. Trust me, when you are in a frustrating situation, your first instinct still may be "Ugh, this is too hard, I can't do this." (Sometimes I still do this!) The difference will be that you will likely catch yourself right after you say or think it and hopefully redirect your thinking. This chapter contains some additional ways that you can stay focused on growth mindsets.

## Secret #20 You Can Help Adults Realize That Mistakes Are Not the End of the World

How you respond to the adults in your lives can actually model growth mindset thinking. (You might be able to teach adults a thing or two about mindsets.) However, before having a conversation with someone about not freaking out about mistakes they make, there is something you always must consider . . . your audience and the timing.

*Know your audience and be very aware of your timing.*

What this warning means is that you should always assess a situation before you say or do something that is important to you. This step is an important one throughout your entire life. Here are some examples of what I mean.

| YOU NOTICE THAT . . . | SO THIS MAY NOT BE AN IDEAL TIME TO . . . |
| --- | --- |
| Your parents just had a very expensive car repair bill right when your sister's college tuition payment was due. | Ask for money or let them know that you need an expensive pair of shoes. |
| Your teacher is not feeling well. | Discuss your grade on an assignment. |
| Your mom is really tired after work each day. | Run around the house with your siblings or friends making a lot of noise. |
| Your coach is not being as patient as he usually is. | Talk with him about playing a different position. |

You should still do the things in the second column if they are important to you—just do them at a more ideal time when the person you need to interact with can give you his or her full attention. Always observe and reflect first.

This is especially important when you want to talk to anyone about growth mindset and why it is important to you. You can share that you have read a book about it or that teachers in school have been discussing it. Let the person know what fixed and growth mindsets are and why growth mindset thinking is important.

So, what are some ways that you can model growth mindset thinking?

A great way is to help other people frame their mistakes in a more positive way. For example, let's say that your mom or dad made a big mistake. Maybe Mom burned the holiday turkey or Dad put a new, bright red T-shirt into the washer, in hot water, with a bunch of white clothes (by mistake), and everything turned pink! They are mad at themselves for making these mistakes, and honestly, you just want to get out their way until they are normal again. Instead of making a beeline to your room, try lightening the mood, being optimistic, and at the same

time, modeling growth mindset thinking by saying something like:

- Good thing that happened; you'll know what to do the next time!
- What a great mistake! That was epic! You will learn tons from that one!
- If you are going to mess up, then you may as well make it a doozy!
- We all learn from our failures.
- This might be a good time to practice a growth mindset.

You can also say these things out loud when you mess up so that you can show adults that mistakes are not the end of the world.

## Secret #21 Accomplish Tasks Yourself

When adults in our life swoop in and do things for us it sort of sends us a message, doesn't it? The message is that they don't think that we can complete the task as fast as they would like us to or that we don't have the capacity to complete the task at all.

Do any of these situations sound familiar?

- Your parent or daycare person runs and grabs your backpack or the bag of stuff you need for after school so that you get to school on time.
- Your parents overhelp with homework.

- Your parents arrange for things that you are supposed to arrange for yourself like your babysitting job or volunteer work.
- Your teacher helps you finish a paper before giving you a chance to figure it out yourself.

Have you ever seen a 2- or 3-year-old have a temper tantrum when someone is trying to help them put their coat on? (I have.) They just want to do it themselves—they want to be independent. Does it feel familiar to you?

Many of the adults in your life just want to help, and they really think they are being helpful in these situations. They don't want to see you struggle, become frustrated, or be late for school or practice. Truth be told, some of you really like that help because that means that you don't have to do it! Challenge yourself to accomplish tasks on your own. It's fine to ask for help, but let adults know that you are able to (and want to) do things yourself. Showing your teachers, parents, and coaches that you want to persevere to complete tasks on your own is another way to model a growth mindset.

## Secret #22 Don't Compare or Compete With Others

Okay, I know, it is a challenge to not compare yourself to your friends or classmates. Trust me, we all have a tendency to want to do this.

Instead of competing with others, compete against yourself. Individually or with your parents, coaches, or teachers, work to set your own goals to accomplish. Don't use others as a goal. What do I mean by that? Instead of setting this goal, "I am going to score more points than my best teammate Patrick," set this goal: "I am going to practice more so that each game, I will score better than my last game." Anything that starts with "I am going to beat (fill in a name) at (fill in an activity)" should be adjusted to "I am going to practice on specific skills so that I can beat my previous performance."

An important part of competing against yourself is that you are the one who sets the goals. This does not mean that you will always meet every goal—in fact, sometimes you will take several steps backward so that you can eventually move forward. Competing with yourself means that you measure your own growth and focus on yourself. (This can also help reduce jealously among friends, classmates, and teammates.) When swimmers try to beat their best time, they are competing with themselves. When high school students retake the SAT or ACT for the second time, they are trying to beat their previous score.

## Secret #23 Play Music to Energize Your Growth Mindset

A really cool hip-hop/rap artist named C. J. Luckey has composed and performed songs and raps that communicate important growth mindset concepts. His single, "The Power of Yet," talks about the importance of process and remaining optimistic. The lyrics communicate that you can cultivate a growth mindset, and even though you are not there yet, you will get there! Other song titles include "Grit and Resilience," "The Famous Mindset," "The Power of Mistakes," and "Praising the Process." Listen to these songs to remind yourself about the importance of having a growth mindset and to help keep you focused and energized. The name of his album is "C.A.P.S." or **C**elebrating **A**ll **P**ersevering **S**tudents. (You can find his songs on iTunes.)

There are a lot of other great songs you might add to a growth mindset playlist too, including:

- "Rise Up" by Audra Day
- "The Climb" by Miley Cyrus
- "It's Not Over Yet" by For King and Country
- "Don't Give Up" by Bruno Mars
- "Try Everything" by Shakira

## Secret #24 Grades Are Not Growth Mindset Friendly

Grades. (Ugh.) Let's face it, grades are not very growth mindset friendly. Think about some recent conversations that you have had with your parents or guardians. Did any of them center around grades on an assignment, test, or report card? Probably. Both kids and adults overemphasize the importance of grades. In fact, sometimes caregivers check online grades so often that they sometimes know how you did on an assignment or assessment before you do! But here's the secret you (and they) need to remember: Grades suggest where you are at one moment of time in one particular subject in one particular skill or concept. Grades do not predict your future, potential, or possibilities. A "bad" grade is an opportunity to reflect, regroup, and relearn. Redoing assignments and retaking tests are all part of a growth mindset!

Grades focus too much on the final product, not the journey to get there. One of the biggest issues with grades is that some of you work really, really hard for a B, C, or D . . . and others of you don't work that hard for an A. A hard-working, persistent kid who earns a C may feel more motivated than a kid who receives an A without a whole lot of effort. Some of you are so busy trying to make the honor roll or get an A that you can lose your love of learning . . . and you never want that to happen! You should be curious about things and learn your entire life!

**ON A SIDE NOTE:**

If your school has a grading system called "standards-based grading" and you don't actually get letter grades (A, B, C, D, and F), then it IS more growth mindset friendly. Either you have mastered the standard or you have not mastered it quite YET.

## Secret #25 Have Some Strategies in Your Back Pocket

This does not actually mean that they are literally in your pocket—it means that you have some go-to strategies to use when you are not understanding something or are stuck. Here are a few that tend to work pretty well in a lot of situations:

— *Think aloud* or *self-talk.* When you are stuck, start thinking aloud about what exactly you are trying to do. This can help you figure out where you might be stuck and identify potential errors in your thinking. Self-talk can also provide us with opportunities to correct errors and move on.

— *Mind mapping.* This is a strategy that maps out your thinking on a piece of paper or through digital software. You can take information that you are learning and transform it into a colorful and organized visual that makes your brain happy. Mind mapping can help you sort out a lot of information in a way that makes sense to you. Start with the concept in the middle of the page and create a visual map from there.

— *Visualize* your neurons connecting as you struggle through a challenge.

— *Look at a previous example* in your book or review any notes that you have taken.

— *Ask a specific question.* Don't say "I don't get this." Start with what you know and then ask a specific question about the part that is confusing you.

I understand that I need to simplify the fraction into the lowest terms, but I can't figure out the next step.

- *Use a highlighter,* sticky note, or something else to "highlight" the most important part of what you are learning.
- *Break the task down into smaller parts.* Some people call this "chunking"—breaking down a lot of information into smaller "chunks" helps you concentrate on learning the information one "chunk" at a time.
- *Take a break.* Scientists have discovered that taking a break once an hour actually increases your productivity and can help us be more creative. If you use the break to be physically active, then even better—it gets your blood flowing and sends more oxygen to your brain!

## Secret #26  Understanding Is More Important Than Speed

When you are learning a new skill, there are times when you just want to learn it fast because you see people around you catching on quickly. (Remember, don't compete with others!) Growth mindset does not focus on how fast you learn anything—the focus is on persevering until you really understand it.

Have you ever had a chance to participate in a Makerspace? (I hope you have—they are awesome spaces where you can build, tinker, and create.) In a Makerspace, you might work on creating something twice as long as anyone else in your group—this means that you had twice the time to problem solve and make mistakes, learn from them, and keep going. Along the way, you have built resilience—so don't get frustrated if it takes you longer to catch on to some things, you will get there and you will have built resiliency along the way.

## Put It All Together

So there you have it, you have just completed reading a book that contained the "secrets" to using a growth mindset. Now go back and look at the first things that you wrote at the beginning of the book—the section that says, "Before you start reading this book . . . " Pay close attention to the responses that you wrote: Are they fixed or growth mindset? Why did you say you were good at the thing you wrote? What were the reasons you wrote about why you considered yourself lousy at something? Could you improve in that area?

Now look at the agree and disagree chart from that first section. Compare your answers with the answers on the next page. Do you know why the responses are fixed or growth?

|  | AGREE OR DISAGREE? | WHY? |
|---|---|---|
| Everyone can learn to draw. | **Disagree**<br>(= *fixed*)<br><br>**Agree**<br>(= *growth*) |  |
| If you practice for long enough, anyone can play varsity sports. | **Disagree**<br>(= *fixed*)<br><br>**Agree**<br>(= *growth*) |  |
| We inherit our weaknesses (like poor math or reading skills) from our parents. | **Disagree**<br>(= *growth*)<br><br>**Agree**<br>(= *fixed*) |  |
| Everyone can learn new things, but some people are just born smarter at certain things than others. | **Disagree**<br>(= *growth*)<br><br>**Agree**<br>(= *fixed*) |  |
| Musical talent is something that you are born with. | **Disagree**<br>(= *growth*)<br><br>**Agree**<br>(= *fixed*) |  |

Coming up next is a section with some "extra" stuff. You will find some other things that will be helpful as well as a list that includes some cool videos and websites. Remember—there is almost nothing that you can't do . . . with the secret power of a growth mindset!

# EXTRAS

Follow Growth Mindset Kids
on Twitter and Facebook

**Twitter:**

@mindsetkid
https://twitter.com/mindsetkid

**Facebook:**

Growth Mindset Kid
https://facebook.com/growth-mindset-kid-
1964566383815071

## Practicing a Growth Mindset

| INSTEAD OF SAYING OR THINKING | YOU COULD SAY |
|---|---|
| It's good enough. | |
| I will never be that smart. | |
| This is too hard. | |
| This is all I can do. | |
| I don't get this. | |
| It's good enough. | |
| Math is not really my thing. | |
| I am not really that smart. | |

# Words to Be Curious About

**All of these are growth mindset words and phrases.**

- tenacity
- grit
- perseverance
- persistence
- stick-to-it-iveness (is that a word?)
- determination
- stamina

- endurance
- staying power
- work ethic
- diligence
- commitment
- drive
- resiliency

**Which words/phrases are very similar in meaning?**

_____

_____

_____

_____

_____

_____

Words to Be Curious About, *Continued.*

**If you had to sort them into two or more categories, how would you do that? What would the categories be?**

_____

_____

_____

_____

_____

**How would you rank them in order of importance?**

_____

_____

_____

_____

_____

Words to Be Curious About, *Continued.*

**How would you rank them in order of their "strength"?**

_____

_____

_____

_____

_____

_____

# Why Do I Need to Learn About My Brain in Order to Have a Growth Mindset? (See Chapter 4)

**Thoughts about this question:**

- Your brain has the ability to get smarter. If we exercise the brain through challenging work and productive struggle, we increase our intelligence.

## People Who Demonstrated Resiliency and Perseverance (Curious? Learn More About Them!)

- Maya Angelou
- Susan B. Anthony
- Walt Disney
- Frederick Douglass
- Milton Hershey
- Leland Melvin

- Simon Rodia
- Sonia Sotomayor
- Harriet Tubman
- Nick Vujicic
- Oprah Winfrey

**Some other people who I think demonstrate a growth mindset:**

_____

_____

_____

_____

_____

_____

# Words From This Book You May Want to Investigate Further

- acceleration
- advocate
- ambidextrous
- capacity
- deliberately
- enrichment
- expectations
- malleable

- meditate
- neuron
- neuroplasticity
- neuroscience
- optimism
- pessimism
- productivity
- prone

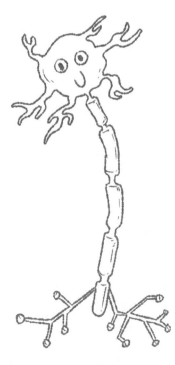

# Some Interesting Websites

### Neuroscience for Kids

http://faculty.washington.edu/chudler/neurok.html
This website includes ideas for science fair projects, memory,
and learning games. It also has some great brain games like
synaptic tag and other outdoor brain games.

### How Stuff Works

http://science.howstuffworks.com/life/inside-the-mind/
human-brain/brain.htm
This site's explanation of the brain and how it works is full of
good information.

### Cosmic Kids

http://www.cosmickids.com
This website has some cool meditation videos.

# Mindset Videos

### *How To Grow Your Brain*

https://www.youtube.com/watch?v=GWSZ1DKjNzY&sns

This Khan Academy video discusses the ways our brain is like a muscle—it requires exercise.

### *Your Brain Is Plastic*

https://www.youtube.com/watch?v=5KLPxDtMqe8

This video provides a great explanation of what happens in our brains when we learn.

### *Brain Jump With Ned the Neuron: Challenges Grow Your Brain*

https://www.youtube.com/watch?v=g7FdMi03CzI

This video reminds you that taking on challenges can grow and strengthen your brain and that you have the power to make your brain stronger every day.

### *Learning—How It Works & How to Do It Better*

https://www.youtube.com/watch?v=u9WpHHJz5Dc

A video that highlights that we learn to do things and that we are not born with knowledge, strengths, and weaknesses. This message is backed up by basic understanding of the brain. We are not "prewired" to do things well—as the video puts it, the babies and butt-kickers learn like "maniacs."

## Mindset Videos, *Continued.*

### Growth Mindset Animation
https://www.youtube.com/watch?v=-_oqghnxBmY&sns

This is a basic introduction to growth and fixed mindsets.

### Stuck on an Escalator
https://www.youtube.com/watch?v=Kq65aAYCHOw

A great video that demonstrates the importance of using strategies when you are stuck on something.

### Perseverance. The Story of Nick Vujicic
https://www.youtube.com/watch?v=gNnVdlvodTQ

This video focuses on the life of Nick Vujicic, a man born with no arms or legs, who demonstrates a growth mindset.

### Famous Failures
https://www.youtube.com/watch?v=zLYECIjmnQs

This video shares the failures of many famous people.

### Shakira–Try Everything
https://www.youtube.com/watch?v=c6rP-YP4c5I

This is the song and video for "Try Everything," a growth mindset song from the movie *Zootopia*.

### C. J. Luckey–The Power of Yet– Official Music Video
https://www.youtube.com/watch?v=J6CnrFvY94E

This music video is all about the Power of Yet.

# No One Is Ever Too Old for Some Good *Sesame Street* Videos

### *Bruno Mars: Don't Give Up*

https://www.youtube.com/watch?v=pWp6kkz-pnQ

Bruno Mars and his Muppet friends sing about the importance of not giving up.

### *Janelle Monae: The Power of Yet*

https://www.youtube.com/watch?v=XLeUvZvuvAs

Janelle Monae sings to her Muppet friends about working hard, staying focused, and eventually getting to where you want to be. That's the "Power of Yet."

### *Elmo Doesn't Give Up Song (Yet Song):*
### *Sesame Street: Little Children, Big Challenges*

https://www.youtube.com/watch?v=vchWYQyZtec

Elmo and a friend sing about how even though Elmo might not be able to do some things right now, he should keep trying.

# Games That Build
## Perseverance and Resiliency

Thinkfun (http://www.thinkfun.com) has a lot of games that can you can play to help develop perseverance and reasoning abilities. My favorites are ShapeOmetry (also called ShapeLogic on Amazon) and Chocolate Fix, but other good ones include:

- Rush Hour

- Color Cube Sudoku

- Gravity Maze

- Circuit Maze

- Block by Block

- Brick by Brick

- Shape by Shape

- Swish

- Laser Maze

- Code Master (fun if you want to learn to code)

- Lunar Landing

# Books

*The Brain:*
*All About Our Nervous System and More!*

by Seymour Simon

*How They Choked:*
*Failures, Flops, and Flaws of the Awfully Famous*

by Georgia Bragg

*Mistakes That Worked:*
*40 Familiar Inventions & How They Came to Be*

by Charlotte Foltz Jones

*The Owner's Manual for Driving Your Adolescent Brain*

by Joann Deak

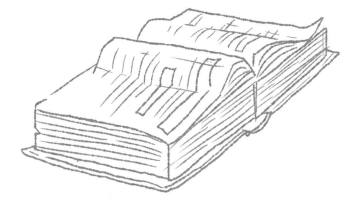

# Growth Mindset Movies

- *Akeelah and the Bee*
- *Apollo 13*
- *A Bug's Life*
- *The Blind Side*
- *Coco*
- *Facing the Giants*
- *Finding Nemo*
- *Forrest Gump*
- *Frozen*
- *Hidden Figures*
- *The Hobbit*

- *Homeward Bound*
- *Inside Out*
- *Leap!*
- *Meet the Robinsons*
- *Mulan*
- *October Sky*
- *Remember the Titans*
- *Soul Surfer*
- *Toy Story*
- *Wonder*
- *Zootopia*

**Can you figure out why these movies made the list?**

## Some Quotes to Think About

66 I don't mind losing as long as I see improvement
or feel I've done as well as I possible could. 99

—Carol Dweck

66 I can accept failure, everyone fails at
something. But I can't accept not trying. 99

—Michael Jordan

66 I have not failed. I've just found
10,000 ways that won't work. 99

—Thomas Edison

66 Failure is a great teacher, and I think when you
make mistakes and you recover from them and
you treat them as valuable learning experiences,
then you've got something to share. 99

—Steve Harvey

66 I don't want the fear of failure to stop me
from doing what I really care about. 99

—Emma Watson

66 I think and think for months and years. Ninety-nine times,
the conclusion is false. The hundredth time I am right. 99

—Albert Einstein

## Some Quotes to Think About, *Continued.*

❝ Enjoy failure and learn from it. You
can never learn from success. ❞

—James Dyson

❝ Failure happens all the time. It happens every day in
practice. What makes you better is how you react to it. ❞

—Mia Hamm

❝ You should never view your challenges as a disadvantage.
Instead, it's more important for you to understand
that your experience facing and overcoming adversity
is actually one of your biggest advantages. ❞

—Michelle Obama

❝ Just try new things. Don't be afraid. Step
out of your comfort zones and soar. ❞

—Michelle Obama

❝ Success is no accident. It is hard work, perseverance,
learning, studying, sacrifice and most of all, love
of what you are doing or learning to do. ❞

—Pele

❝ Perseverance is not a long race; it is many
short races one after the other. ❞

—Walter Elliott

## Some Quotes to Think About, *Continued.*

**Give it a try! Create your own quotes for the following:**

*Perseverance:*

_____

_____

*Resiliency:*

_____

_____

*Learning From Mistakes:*

_____

_____

*Goal-Setting:*

_____

_____

# Quotes I Used in This Book

❝ It is a mistake to think that the practice of my art has become easy to me. I assure you, dear friend, no one has given so much care to the study of composition as I. There is scarcely a famous master in music whose works I have not frequently and diligently studied. ❞

—Wolfgang Amadeus Mozart, from *Mozart: The Man and the Artist Revealed in His Own Words* by Friedrich Kerst and Henry Krehbiel

❝ It is impossible to live without failing at something. ❞

—J. K. Rowling, speech given June 5, 2008, at Harvard, titled "The Fringe Benefits of Failing and the Importance of Imagination"

# ABOUT THE AUTHOR

**Mary Cay Ricci** used to be a fixed mindset kid (she still has to fight a fixed mindset when it comes to some things—like sports). Now she is a growth mindset mom of three kids and one pooch. She was also an elementary and middle school teacher and has written books about mindsets for teachers and parents.